To my daughter, Farris Christine, to whom the mantle of these principles is passing.
I pray that God's strength and wisdom will always radiate your mind, body, spirit, and soul.
You are a brilliant light in the world. Be bold and beautiful. Love will see you through!

—A. F. W.

To my partner in life, Allan, who knows better than anyone that love will see you through

—S. W. C.

ACKNOWLEDGMENTS

The inspiration for this book came from many special people in my life:
My uncle Martin Luther King Jr., who created a vital lesson on the power of love.
My parents, Isaac and Christine Farris, who love me unconditionally.
My grandparents Rev. Dr. and Mrs. Martin Luther King Sr., who gave so much and loved even more.
My spiritual mentor, Apostle Darryl L. Winston, who helps to open my spirit and navigate the journey well.
My agent, Jennifer Lyons, who encourages me to write.

SIMON & SCHUSTER BOOKS FOR YOUNG READERS • An imprint of Simon & Schuster Children's Publishing Division • 1230 Avenue of the Americas, New York, New York 10020 • Text copyright © 2015 by Angela Farris Watkins • Illustrations copyright © 2015 by Sally Wern Comport • All rights reserved, including the right of reproduction in whole or in part in any form. • SIMON & SCHUSTER BOOKS FOR YOUNG READERS is a trademark of Simon & Schuster, Inc. • For information about special discounts for bulk purchases, please contact Simon & Schuster Special Sales at 1-866-506-1949 or business@simonandschuster .com. • The Simon & Schuster Speakers Bureau can bring authors to your live event. For more information or to book an event, contact the Simon & Schuster Speakers Bureau at 1-866-248-3049 or visit our website at www.simonspeakers.com. • Book design by Laurent Linn • The text for this book is set in Minister Std. • The illustrations for this book are rendered in mixed media, including traditional charcoal drawing, acrylic paint, and tissue- and cut-paper collage, as well as digital drawing, painting, and collage. • Manufactured in China • 1014 SCP • 10 9 8 7 6 5 4 3 2 1 • Library of Congress Cataloging-in-Publication Data • Watkins, Angela Farris. • Love will see you through : Martin Luther King Jr.'s six guiding beliefs (as told by his niece) / Angela Farris Watkins ; illustrated by Sally Wern Comport — 1st ed. • p. cm. • ISBN 978-1-4169-8693-5 (hardcover) • 1. King, Martin Luther, Jr., 1929–1968—Philosophy—Juvenile literature. 2. King, Martin Luther, Jr., 1929–1968—Juvenile literature. I. Comport, Sally Wern, illustrator. • II. Title. • E185.97.K5W327 2015 • 323.092—dc22 • 2009049991

first edition

Love Will See You Through

MARTIN LUTHER KING JR.'S SIX GUIDING BELIEFS
(as told by his niece)

Angela Farris Watkins, PhD

ILLUSTRATED BY Sally Wern Comport

SIMON & SCHUSTER BOOKS FOR YOUNG READERS

New York   London   Toronto   Sydney   New Delhi

Martin Luther King Jr.

is recognized as one of the greatest men in history.

I'm proud to say that he was also my uncle.

Uncle Martin worked hard to end segregation and discrimination against African Americans. As he did so, Uncle Martin helped make America better.

He believed that love and nonviolence were the solution. They were the basis of his six guiding beliefs.

Uncle Martin faced adversity with courage. For him, courage meant solving problems without using violence. In 1955, Uncle Martin led a boycott to address the problem of segregation that forced African Americans to ride in the back of or stand up on public buses in Montgomery, Alabama. He encouraged people to stop riding the buses until segregation on buses ended.

One night, as Uncle Martin spoke at a local church in Montgomery, he got the news that his house had been bombed by people who were angry about the boycott. He knew that his wife and two-month-old baby girl were inside the house. Uncle Martin rushed home.

There he found a mass of policemen, news reporters, and fire trucks surrounding his house. There were also many African Americans who wanted him to fight back.

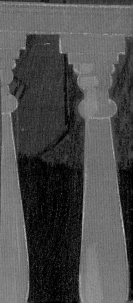

Uncle Martin courageously resisted the use of violence that night. First Uncle Martin made sure that his family was safe. Then he walked onto his front porch and told the people to put down their weapons. He explained that the bus boycott would be won only with a spirit of love.

Uncle Martin was right. In December of the following year he proudly announced that segregation on Montgomery's buses was over.

2: LOVE your Enemies

Uncle Martin believed that as we courageously face our problems, we must seek to love our enemies. One Sunday morning Uncle Martin preached a sermon called "Loving Your Enemies."

In his sermon Uncle Martin explained *how* to love our enemies and *why* we must love our enemies. He said that first we must make sure that we have love in our hearts. Then we should realize that there is good and bad in everyone. Uncle Martin said that we should find the good in our enemies and love that part of them.

Uncle Martin said that the reason *why* we must love our enemies is because God wants us to. He also said that the more people hate, the more we will all live in a world filled with hate. Hate eventually destroys the spirit and the mind of the person who holds it.

But love makes everyone stronger.

3: Fight the Pro Not the Person Who Caused It

Uncle Martin fought his problems without fighting people. He believed that if you love your enemies, you can focus all your energy on solving the problem. Just before Easter Sunday in 1963, Uncle Martin went to Birmingham, Alabama, to stop segregation against African Americans in stores and restaurants there. He was arrested and put in jail for protesting.

As he read the local newspaper, he discovered a letter by some of his fellow preachers and pastors. In it they said that his protests in Birmingham were untimely and that he should back away.

Uncle Martin wrote a letter in response that did not attack the preachers and pastors but rather focused on the problem of segregation. In the letter, he expressed his love and respect for the ministers. He knew that his letter was an opportunity to explain to hundreds of people why the battle for equality must be fought. Uncle Martin's letter received a lot of public attention and became famously known as the "Letter from Birmingham Jail."

4: When Innocent People Are Hurt, Others Are Inspired to Help

Uncle Martin believed that when undeserving people are hurt, it inspires others to offer their help. He demonstrated this when he went to Selma, Alabama, in 1965 to organize a voter registration drive and to stop discrimination that prevented African Americans from registering to vote.

After Uncle Martin successfully registered to vote at a local Selma hotel, a white man attacked him because he didn't want African Americans to vote. Many of the people who fought for the voting rights of African Americans were also beaten as they marched and protested. When the world saw this cruelty and hatred, they witnessed the real evil behind discrimination.

Across the country, people stepped forward to offer their help. President Lyndon B. Johnson was one of those people. Uncle Martin spoke with the president by phone. Later that year President Johnson signed the Voting Rights Act, which outlawed discrimination in voter registration throughout the United States.

5: Resist

Uncle Martin believed that we are all connected to one another. If someone hurts another person, they are also hurting themselves.

Violence of Any Kind

He also understood that violence is a destructive force, but that love has the power to create and build. So even when Uncle Martin was hurt, he did not respond with violence.

In 1966 he went to Chicago to protest practices that kept African Americans from having the same kind of housing as white people. As he and others marched, someone who hated his protest threw a rock that hit him in the head. Uncle Martin fell down on one knee for several moments. He didn't yell out, throw the rock back, or encourage his supporters to fight back. He knew that responding with violence would destroy his chances of creating better housing for African Americans.

Uncle Martin got back up and continued the march. With a spirit of love, he stayed focused and kept working. Later that year the real estate board, housing authority, and banking institutions of Chicago all agreed to stop housing discrimination toward African Americans.

6: The Universe Honors LOVE

Uncle Martin believed that a higher force in the universe honors us when we use love. He put a lot of love out into the universe, and the universe honored him by giving him the power to achieve great things. Although he lived his life in constant danger, he refused violence because he knew love would prevail.

Though Uncle Martin was killed by an act of violence, people have honored his legacy of love. The name Martin Luther King Jr. is recognized all over the world. A national holiday is named for him and celebrated every year. Countless city streets are named after him. All over the world, buildings and memorials stand in tribute to him.

But more important than any of that, America is a better place because of Uncle Martin!

Uncle Martin was a man of peace.

Love was his way of life.

Uncle Martin's six guiding beliefs teach us that love has power.

His life was proof that . . .